RAGDOLLS

by Gini Holland

New York

Published in 2014 by The Rosen Publishing Group, Inc.
29 East 21st Street, New York, NY 10010

Produced for Rosen by Ruby Tuesday Books Ltd
Editor for Ruby Tuesday Books Ltd: Mark J. Sachner
US Editor: Sara Howell
Designer: Emma Randall

Photo Credits:
Cover, 1, 4–5, 6–7, 8–9, 11, 13, 14–15, 16–17, 18–19, 20–21, 24–25, 30 © Shutterstock; 10 © Cassia Afini/Wikipedia Creative Commons; 23, 27 © Alamy; 29 © Stan Honda/Getty Images.

Library of Congress Cataloging-in-Publication Data

Holland, Gini.
 Ragdolls / by Gini Holland.
    pages cm. — (Cats are cool)
 Includes index.
 ISBN 978-1-4777-1276-4 (library binding) — ISBN 978-1-4777-1340-2 (pbk.) —
 ISBN 978-1-4777-1341-9 (6-pack)
 1. Ragdoll cat—Juvenile literature. I. Title.
 SF449.R34H65 2014
 636.8—dc23
                                    2013002106

Manufactured in the United States of America

CPSIA Compliance Information: Batch #:S13PK7 For Further Information contact: Rosen Publishing, New York, New York at 1-800-237-9932

Contents

A Cat, a Doll, or a Puppy?

Have you ever held a floppy cloth doll? That's what a ragdoll cat feels like when you pick it up. Ragdolls go limp like dolls made of rags. That's how they got their name.

Ragdolls love to be with people. Sometimes people even call them "puppy cats." That's because they will follow people from room to room, just like puppies.

Ragdolls are big cats! They weigh between 15 and 20 pounds (7–9 kg) when they are grown up. They have big bones and strong muscles that help them carry all that weight around.

A ragdoll cat

Perfect Purr Facts

Some people call ragdolls "cuddly cats," because they are soft, friendly, and fun to snuggle with.

Brand New Cats!

Some **breeds** of cats are thousands of years old. A ragdoll, however, is a fairly new kind of cat. It is only about 60 years old.

The ragdoll breed started in the 1960s in Riverside, California. A cat **breeder** named Ann Baker met her neighbor's cat, Josephine. Josephine had long, white fur and blue eyes. It's believed she was a mixture of two breeds, Persian and Angora.

Ann noticed that Josephine loved to be cuddled.

Blue eyes

Short muzzle

When Josephine had kittens, Ann bought some of the kittens from her neighbor. She decided she would use the kittens to create a special breed of extra cuddly cats.

An adult Angora cat

A four-month-old Persian kitten

Perfect Purr Facts

Persian cats have long hair, round faces, and short **muzzles**. They can have white fur and sometimes have blue eyes. Angoras have medium to long white fur and often have blue eyes.

The First Ragdolls

Josephine's kittens had medium to long, soft fur. They felt as soft as bunnies. They also liked to be held!

Josephine's kittens relaxed and got floppy in people's arms. They also liked to spend time with people. As long as people played with them, these cats were happy.

Ann Baker waited until Josephine's kittens grew up. Then she began her plan of breeding the kittens. Ann also bred more kittens from Josephine. She chose **mates** for Josephine that had blue eyes. Some of these male cats also had pale fur with dark areas known as **points**.

Over time, Ann was able to breed cats that look like the ragdoll cats we see today. In fact, all true ragdolls come from Josephine and her kittens.

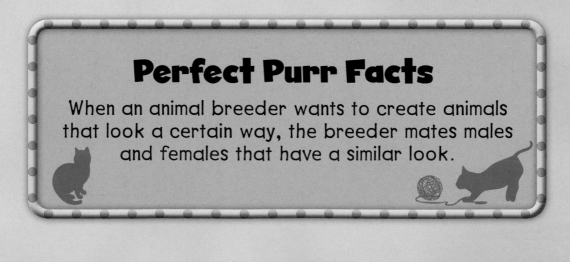

Perfect Purr Facts

When an animal breeder wants to create animals that look a certain way, the breeder mates males and females that have a similar look.

Ragdoll kittens

Points

Points

Perfect Points

Ann Baker carefully bred ragdolls to make big, loving animals that have light-colored fur with darker points. Now, because of her work, the ragdoll is a "pointed" breed.

Pointed cats have fur on their tail, legs, and feet that is darker than their body color. They also have a dark mask over their faces and dark ears. A ragdoll's points can be dark brown, which is called seal, or chocolate, which is a paler brown. They can also be dark cream or a pale ginger that is called flame. Points can also be lilac, which is a frosty gray with a hint of pink, or a color called blue, which isn't actually blue, but gray. Some ragdolls even have points that are stripy or blotchy.

A ragdoll kitten with flame points

Perfect Purr Facts

A ragdoll cat with lynx points has dark and light stripes on its points. A cat with tortie points has splotches of colors on its points. Some ragdolls have the lynx and tortie patterns together.

A ragdoll with lynx points

A Mix of Colors and Patterns

A ragdoll's fur can be white, ivory, bluish white, cream, and a very pale brown called fawn.

Ragdolls usually come in three main patterns. The patterns are color point, mitted, and bicolor. Color point ragdolls have a body in one color with darker points.

A mitted ragdoll is colored like a color point, but it has white front paws that look like mittens. It also has white back legs a white chin, and a white belly stripe.

Bicolors only have dark coloring on their tails, ears, and edges of their masks. They have white feet, chests, and bellies, and may have splashes of white or their point color on their backs.

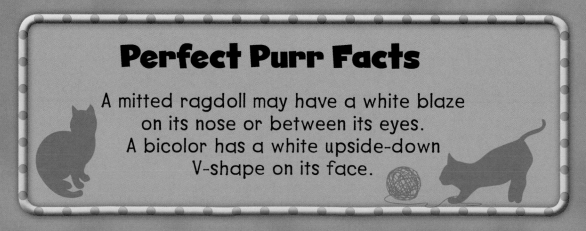

Perfect Purr Facts

A mitted ragdoll may have a white blaze on its nose or between its eyes. A bicolor has a white upside-down V-shape on its face.

A color point
kitten with
seal-colored
points

White blaze

White mittens

A mitted ragdoll

Upside-down white V

A bicolor ragdoll with blue
point coloring

13

More Ragdoll Looks

With their mixtures of different fur colors, point colors, and patterns, beautiful ragdolls have many different looks. Some breeders even breed a type of ragdoll that doesn't have points. These cats are called solid ragdolls.

Don't be fooled by the name, though! Solid ragdolls don't have one solid body color. These ragdolls have less light fur than other ragdolls and instead of points, they have solid patches of darker fur. The dark fur of a solid ragdoll can come in many colors including black.

Ragdolls usually have blue eyes, but the eyes of solid ragdolls can be green, **aqua**, or copper. Sometimes, these cats even have a different color for each eye!

A solid ragdoll

Perfect Purr Facts

There is another type of ragdoll called the mink ragdoll. It is called a mink because its fur is so soft and thick it feels like a mink fur coat.

Magical Newborn Kittens

Pointed ragdoll kittens are born white. After a few weeks, like magic, color markings start to show on their ears, legs, face, and tail.

As the kittens grow up, these marks get darker. Eventually, the marks darken to form the seal, chocolate, blue, lilac, flame, or dark cream points that the cat will have for the rest of its life. Solid or mink ragdoll kittens don't have to wait until they grow up. They are born with their full coloring.

Ragdoll kittens come in lots of colors and patterns, but all of them are floppy and friendly.

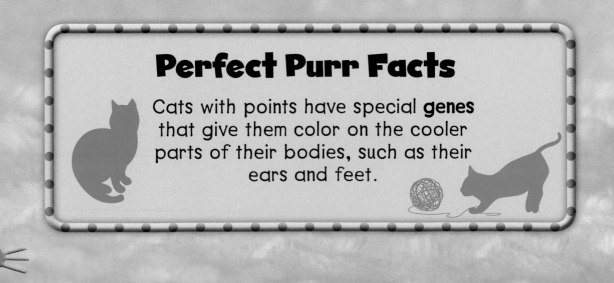

Perfect Purr Facts

Cats with points have special **genes** that give them color on the cooler parts of their bodies, such as their ears and feet.

The dark points on these ragdoll kittens are just starting to appear.

Ragdoll Kittens Grow Up

Newborn ragdoll kittens drink milk from their mothers. At about four weeks of age, most ragdolls are ready for **solid food.** You can tell, because they will start chewing on things!

At this age, the kittens will eat a little kitten food, but they will still nurse from their mother.

At about 12 weeks old, most ragdolls are ready to go to a new home. If you adopt a kitten, keep it in one room at first. You don't want to lose it in your house! It will like a little basket to sleep in and a **litter box** it can get in and out of. After a few days, you can let it explore more of your house.

Perfect Purr Facts

Like adult ragdolls, kittens like to snuggle and play with people, so spend plenty of time with your kitten. It will also enjoy playing with toys that move.

Honestly, it was like this when I found it!

This is a great hiding place!

It's been a tiring day.

19

Ragdolls Take Their Time

Ragdolls are big cats, but they start small and grow slowly. That's why most breeders won't let a kitten go to its new home until it is at least 12 weeks old. Until then, a ragdoll kitten needs to be close to its mother.

Ragdolls usually reach their full size and weight when they are about four years old. Males usually stop growing at 15 to 20 pounds (7–9 kg). Females are smaller, and they usually weigh between 10 and 15 pounds (4.5–7 kg).

Pointed ragdolls don't get their full color until they are two years old. This means you can watch these cats slowly darken and change color as they grow up.

An adult ragdoll with bright blue eyes

Perfect Purr Facts

Every breed of kitten is born with blue eyes, but the eye color of many types of cats changes as the kitten grows up. The eyes of most ragdoll cats do not change color as they get older, however. They stay bright blue for their whole lives.

A blue-eyed ragdoll kitten

Bath Time for Ragdolls!

Some ragdolls will let you place them in warm baths. They will just lie there and let you soap them up and rinse them off.

Some ragdolls will even let you dry them with blow dryers! Others, however, hate water, blow dryers, and vacuums, just as other cats do. Luckily, ragdolls **groom** themselves well. Many don't ever need a bath.

Most longhaired cats have an **undercoat** of short fur under their long hair. Ragdolls have medium-long hair, but they don't have much of an undercoat. This helps keep ragdolls' fur from getting very **matted**. Their owners may only have to brush them once or twice a week. Other breeds of longhaired cats may need brushing more often.

Perfect Purr Facts

If a ragdoll needs a bath, it should be brushed first, just in case it has mats, or lumpy tangles, in its fur. Mats are harder to get out once they are wet.

A ragdoll being groomed by its owner

23

Friends, Not Fighters

Don't count on a ragdoll to catch mice or keep rabbits out of your yard. Ragdolls like to play, but they do not like to hunt.

In fact, ragdolls are so gentle that they are safer when kept indoors. They may not fight off another cat or dog. They could get into trouble outside, unless someone is with them to protect them at all times.

When a ragdoll plays, it doesn't extend its claws. Once in a while, however, a ragdoll might bite. This is **rare**. Sometimes it means someone is playing too roughly with it. Often, it means the ragdoll is not getting enough attention.

Perfect Purr Facts

The best way to teach a ragdoll to stop biting is to say "No" firmly, and then gently put it in a room by itself for a little while. It does not like to be alone, so it will learn quickly.

A ragdoll cat spends some time outside with its owner.

25

Fancy Cats and Cat Fanciers

When Ann Baker started her breed, she wanted a cat club just for ragdolls. She began the Ragdoll Society in 1975.

Now the club is called the Ragdoll Fanciers Club International, or RFCI. A cat fancier is someone who likes cats.

Each year, people from all over the world show their ragdolls at the RFCI cat show. Lucky cats are judged the Best Champion, Best Alter, and Best Kitten. Best Alters are cats that are **altered** so they can't have kittens. The RFCI Best Champion for 2011 was a cream-pointed cat named Pidepipurr Von Halen.

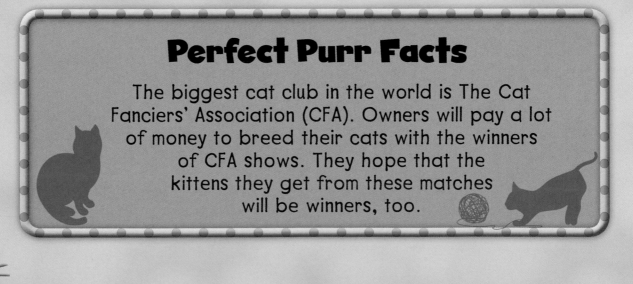

Perfect Purr Facts

The biggest cat club in the world is The Cat Fanciers' Association (CFA). Owners will pay a lot of money to breed their cats with the winners of CFA shows. They hope that the kittens they get from these matches will be winners, too.

This owner is showing off his beautiful ragdoll kitten at a cat show.

From a Box to a Fancy Hotel

One lucky ragdoll named Matilda lives in the Algonquin Hotel in New York City.

Matilda was found in a box and rescued when she was just a kitten. Now, she likes to sit on the front desk and welcome people when they come into the lobby.

People love Matilda. She was recently named "Cat of the Year" at the Westchester Cat Show in Westchester County, New York. Her picture is on a children's book and also on a Christmas ornament. The hotel has even named a drink after her!

As you might expect, Matilda has over five thousand followers on Facebook. She is one popular cat and she is not alone. All over the world, ragdoll fans will tell you that these big, soft, cuddly cats are the best and coolest cats around!

Matilda sits on the front desk in the Algonquin Hotel's lobby.

Perfect Purr Facts

The Algonquin Hotel has kept a cat in its lobby since the 1930s. Its male cats are always named Hamlet, and its female cats are always called Matilda.

Glossary

altered (OL-terd) An animal that has had an operation so it cannot have babies.

aqua (AH-kwuh) A light blue-green color.

breeds (BREEDZ) Types of cats or other animals. Also, the word used to describe the act of mating two animals in order to produce young.

breeder (BREED-er) A person who breeds animals and sells them.

genes (JEENZ) Structures that make a code in the body that says what eye color, hair color, and all other kinds of body parts an animal or person will have.

groom (GROOM) To clean by licking, washing, or brushing.

ivory (EYEV-ree) A creamy-white color.

litter box (LIH-ter BOKS) A shallow plastic box or tray filled with stony or sandy material that a cat uses as a bathroom.

mates (MAYTS) The partner an animal produces its young with. Also, to put a male and female animal together so they produce young.

matted (MAT-ed) Fur or hair that is so tangled that it looks like cloth and is hard to brush.

muzzles (MUH-zelz) The nose and mouth areas of a cat, dog, and many other mammals.

points (POYNTZ) The colored face, tail, feet, legs, and ears of a cat with a light body.

rare (RER) Something that only happens once in a long while.

solid food (SOH-led FOOD) Food that is not a liquid, such as meat or canned kitten food.

undercoat (UN-der-koht) The short hair or fur that can lie under an animal's longer hair.

Websites

Due to the changing nature of Internet links, PowerKids Press has developed an online list of websites related to the subject of this book. This site is updated regularly. Please use this link to access the list:

www.powerkidslinks.com/cac/rag

Read More

Landau, Elaine. *Ragdolls Are the Best!*. Best Cats Ever. Minneapolis, MN: Lerner Publishing Group, 2011.

Micco, Trudy. *Discover Ragdoll Cats*. Discover Cats with the Cat Fanciers' Association. Berkeley Heights, NJ: Enslow Elementary, 2013.

Wheeler, Jill C. *Ragdoll Cats*. Checkerboard Animal Library: Cats. Minneapolis, MN: Checkerboard Books, 2012.

Index